50 Greece Ice Cream Recipes

By: Kelly Johnson

Table of Contents

- Baklava Ice Cream
- Greek Yogurt and Honey Ice Cream
- Pistachio Gelato
- Loukoumades (Greek Honey Donut) Ice Cream
- Masticha Ice Cream (Mastic-flavored)
- Greek Coffee Ice Cream
- Lemon and Feta Ice Cream
- Rosewater Sorbet
- Orange and Almond Gelato
- Greek Vanilla Ice Cream with Mastiha
- Pomegranate and Mint Sorbet
- Fig and Honey Gelato
- Karydopita (Greek Walnut Cake) Ice Cream
- Kousmis (Greek Lemon Sorbet)
- Yogurt and Strawberry Gelato
- Cucumber and Mint Sorbet
- Watermelon and Feta Ice Cream

- Cinnamon and Clove Greek Ice Cream
- Choco-Baklava Swirl Ice Cream
- Apricot and Greek Yogurt Sorbet
- Almond and Honey Ice Cream
- Greek-style Cinnamon and Honey Gelato
- Pistachio and Rosewater Gelato
- Mastiha Pine Nut Ice Cream
- Orange Blossom Ice Cream
- Pomegranate and Yogurt Gelato
- Chocolate and Olive Oil Gelato
- Greek Saffron Ice Cream
- Almond Fig Sorbet
- Greek Yogurt and Blueberry Gelato
- Karydopita Ice Cream Sandwich
- Cherry and Ricotta Gelato
- Zymar (Greek Apricot and Yogurt) Sorbet
- Coconut and Lemon Gelato
- Honey and Lavender Ice Cream
- Grape and Ouzo Sorbet

- Cretan Honeycomb Ice Cream
- Choco-Hazelnut and Yogurt Gelato
- Greek Spice Cake Ice Cream
- Greek Yogurt and Peach Sorbet
- Strawberry and Feta Ice Cream
- Fresh Lime and Olive Oil Sorbet
- Hazelnut and Cinnamon Gelato
- Watermelon and Mint Gelato
- Baklava-Inspired Nut Gelato
- Lemon and Yogurt Cheesecake Ice Cream
- Raspberry and Pistachio Ice Cream
- Chocolate-Orange Greek Yogurt Gelato
- Mastiha Lemonade Sorbet
- Cinnamon-Orange Almond Gelato

Baklava Ice Cream

Ingredients:

- 2 cups heavy cream
- 1 cup whole milk
- 1 cup Greek yogurt
- 1/2 cup honey
- 1 tsp vanilla extract
- 1/2 cup crushed pistachios
- 1/2 cup crushed walnuts
- 1/2 tsp ground cinnamon
- 2 tbsp sugar (optional)

Instructions:

1. In a mixing bowl, whisk together the heavy cream, whole milk, Greek yogurt, honey, vanilla extract, and sugar until smooth.
2. In a separate bowl, mix the crushed pistachios, walnuts, and cinnamon.
3. Add the nut mixture into the cream mixture and stir to combine.
4. Pour the mixture into an ice cream maker and churn according to the manufacturer's instructions.
5. Transfer the ice cream to a container and freeze for 4-6 hours or until firm.
6. Serve with a drizzle of honey and extra crushed pistachios or walnuts.

Greek Yogurt and Honey Ice Cream

Ingredients:

- 2 cups Greek yogurt
- 1 cup heavy cream
- 1/2 cup honey
- 1 tsp vanilla extract
- 1/4 cup water (optional for thinning)

Instructions:

1. In a bowl, whisk together the Greek yogurt, heavy cream, honey, and vanilla extract until smooth.
2. If the mixture is too thick, add a little water to thin it out to your desired consistency.
3. Pour the mixture into an ice cream maker and churn according to the manufacturer's instructions.
4. Transfer the ice cream to a container and freeze for at least 4 hours or until firm.
5. Serve with additional honey drizzled on top.

Pistachio Gelato

Ingredients:

- 1 cup shelled pistachios
- 2 cups whole milk
- 1 cup heavy cream
- 3/4 cup sugar
- 1 tsp vanilla extract
- Pinch of salt

Instructions:

1. In a blender or food processor, pulse the pistachios into a fine paste.
2. In a saucepan, heat the milk and heavy cream over medium heat, stirring occasionally.
3. In a separate bowl, whisk the sugar and salt together. Gradually add the sugar to the milk mixture and stir until dissolved.
4. Stir in the pistachio paste and vanilla extract, then simmer for 5-7 minutes.
5. Let the mixture cool to room temperature, then refrigerate for 2 hours or until chilled.
6. Pour the chilled mixture into an ice cream maker and churn according to the manufacturer's instructions.
7. Freeze for at least 4 hours before serving.

Loukoumades (Greek Honey Donut) Ice Cream

Ingredients:

- 2 cups heavy cream
- 1 cup whole milk
- 1/2 cup Greek yogurt
- 1/2 cup honey
- 1 tsp vanilla extract
- 1/2 tsp cinnamon
- 1/2 cup mini loukoumades (small honey donuts, store-bought or homemade)
- 1 tbsp chopped walnuts (optional)

Instructions:

1. In a mixing bowl, combine the heavy cream, whole milk, Greek yogurt, honey, vanilla extract, and cinnamon.
2. Whisk until smooth and refrigerate for 2-3 hours to chill.
3. Once chilled, pour the mixture into an ice cream maker and churn according to the manufacturer's instructions.
4. During the last few minutes of churning, add in the mini loukoumades and walnuts (if using).
5. Transfer the ice cream to a container and freeze for 4-6 hours before serving.

Masticha Ice Cream (Mastic-flavored)

Ingredients:

- 2 cups heavy cream
- 1 cup whole milk
- 3 tbsp mastic resin (or 1 tsp mastic extract)
- 3/4 cup sugar
- 1 tsp vanilla extract

Instructions:

1. In a small bowl, grind the mastic resin into a fine powder using a mortar and pestle or spice grinder.
2. In a saucepan, heat the milk, heavy cream, and sugar over medium heat, stirring occasionally.
3. Once the mixture is warm, add the mastic powder and vanilla extract. Stir to combine, ensuring the mastic dissolves.
4. Remove the mixture from heat and let it cool to room temperature.
5. Refrigerate for at least 2 hours or until chilled.
6. Pour the chilled mixture into an ice cream maker and churn according to the manufacturer's instructions.
7. Freeze for at least 4 hours before serving.

Greek Coffee Ice Cream

Ingredients:

- 2 cups heavy cream
- 1 cup whole milk
- 1/2 cup sugar
- 2 tbsp finely ground Greek coffee (or espresso powder)
- 1 tsp vanilla extract

Instructions:

1. In a saucepan, heat the milk and heavy cream over medium heat. Add the sugar and stir until dissolved.
2. Once the mixture is warm, add the ground coffee and stir until fully dissolved.
3. Remove from heat and let the mixture cool to room temperature. Then, refrigerate for 2 hours or until chilled.
4. Once chilled, pour the mixture into an ice cream maker and churn according to the manufacturer's instructions.
5. Freeze for at least 4 hours before serving.

Lemon and Feta Ice Cream

Ingredients:

- 1 cup heavy cream
- 1 cup whole milk
- 1/2 cup crumbled feta cheese
- 1/2 cup sugar
- 1/2 cup lemon juice
- Zest of 1 lemon

Instructions:

1. In a blender, combine the heavy cream, whole milk, crumbled feta cheese, sugar, lemon juice, and lemon zest.
2. Blend until smooth and refrigerate for 2 hours to chill.
3. Once chilled, pour the mixture into an ice cream maker and churn according to the manufacturer's instructions.
4. Freeze for at least 4 hours before serving.

Rosewater Sorbet

Ingredients:

- 2 cups water
- 1 cup sugar
- 1/4 cup rosewater
- 1/2 cup lemon juice

Instructions:

1. In a saucepan, combine water and sugar, heating over medium heat until the sugar is dissolved.
2. Remove from heat and stir in the rosewater and lemon juice.
3. Let the mixture cool to room temperature, then refrigerate for 2-3 hours.
4. Once chilled, pour the mixture into an ice cream maker and churn according to the manufacturer's instructions.
5. Freeze for at least 4 hours before serving.

Orange and Almond Gelato

Ingredients:

- 2 cups whole milk
- 1 cup heavy cream
- 1/2 cup sugar
- Zest of 2 oranges
- 1/4 cup orange juice
- 1/2 cup almond meal
- 1 tsp almond extract
- 1/4 tsp vanilla extract

Instructions:

1. In a saucepan, heat the milk and heavy cream over medium heat, stirring occasionally.
2. Add the sugar, orange zest, and orange juice. Stir to dissolve the sugar.
3. Remove from heat and let it cool for 15-20 minutes.
4. Whisk in the almond meal, almond extract, and vanilla extract until smooth.
5. Refrigerate the mixture for 2-3 hours until chilled.
6. Once chilled, pour into an ice cream maker and churn according to the manufacturer's instructions.
7. Freeze for at least 4 hours before serving.

Greek Vanilla Ice Cream with Mastiha

Ingredients:

- 2 cups heavy cream
- 1 cup whole milk
- 3/4 cup sugar
- 2 tsp mastiha resin (or mastic extract)
- 1 tsp vanilla extract
- Pinch of salt

Instructions:

1. Grind the mastiha resin into a fine powder using a mortar and pestle.
2. In a saucepan, heat the milk, heavy cream, sugar, and salt over medium heat.
3. Once warm, add the mastiha powder and stir until dissolved.
4. Remove from heat and let the mixture cool to room temperature, then refrigerate for 2-3 hours to chill.
5. Once chilled, pour into an ice cream maker and churn according to the manufacturer's instructions.
6. Freeze for at least 4 hours before serving.

Pomegranate and Mint Sorbet

Ingredients:

- 2 cups pomegranate juice
- 1/2 cup sugar
- 1/4 cup fresh mint leaves
- 1 tbsp lemon juice

Instructions:

1. In a saucepan, heat the pomegranate juice and sugar over medium heat until the sugar is dissolved.
2. Remove from heat and stir in the fresh mint leaves. Let steep for 10 minutes.
3. Strain the mixture to remove the mint leaves, then add the lemon juice.
4. Let the mixture cool to room temperature, then refrigerate for 2-3 hours.
5. Once chilled, pour into an ice cream maker and churn according to the manufacturer's instructions.
6. Freeze for at least 4 hours before serving.

Fig and Honey Gelato

Ingredients:

- 2 cups whole milk
- 1 cup heavy cream
- 1/2 cup honey
- 1 cup dried figs, chopped
- 1 tsp vanilla extract

Instructions:

1. In a saucepan, heat the milk and heavy cream over medium heat until warm.
2. Add the honey and chopped figs, stirring to dissolve the honey.
3. Simmer for 5-10 minutes, then remove from heat and let the mixture steep for 30 minutes.
4. Strain out the figs, then stir in the vanilla extract.
5. Let the mixture cool to room temperature, then refrigerate for 2-3 hours.
6. Once chilled, pour into an ice cream maker and churn according to the manufacturer's instructions.
7. Freeze for at least 4 hours before serving.

Karydopita (Greek Walnut Cake) Ice Cream

Ingredients:

- 2 cups whole milk
- 1 cup heavy cream
- 3/4 cup sugar
- 1/2 cup crushed walnuts
- 1 tsp cinnamon
- 1/2 tsp nutmeg
- 1 tsp vanilla extract
- 1/4 cup honey

Instructions:

1. In a saucepan, heat the milk and heavy cream over medium heat until warm.
2. Stir in the sugar, cinnamon, nutmeg, and vanilla extract, dissolving the sugar completely.
3. Add the crushed walnuts and honey, then simmer for 5 minutes.
4. Remove from heat and let cool to room temperature. Strain out the walnuts and refrigerate for 2-3 hours.
5. Once chilled, pour into an ice cream maker and churn according to the manufacturer's instructions.
6. Freeze for at least 4 hours before serving.

Kousmis (Greek Lemon Sorbet)

Ingredients:

- 2 cups water
- 1 cup sugar
- 1 cup fresh lemon juice
- Zest of 2 lemons
- 1 tbsp lemon zest

Instructions:

1. In a saucepan, combine water and sugar, heating over medium heat until the sugar dissolves.
2. Remove from heat and stir in the fresh lemon juice and zest.
3. Let the mixture cool to room temperature, then refrigerate for 2-3 hours.
4. Once chilled, pour the mixture into an ice cream maker and churn according to the manufacturer's instructions.
5. Freeze for at least 4 hours before serving.

Yogurt and Strawberry Gelato

Ingredients:

- 1 1/2 cups Greek yogurt
- 1 cup heavy cream
- 1 cup fresh strawberries, chopped
- 1/2 cup sugar
- 1 tsp vanilla extract

Instructions:

1. In a saucepan, heat the strawberries and sugar over medium heat until the strawberries release their juice.
2. Mash the strawberries and simmer for 5 minutes, then remove from heat and let cool.
3. In a bowl, combine the Greek yogurt, heavy cream, vanilla extract, and cooled strawberry mixture.
4. Whisk until smooth and refrigerate for 2-3 hours.
5. Once chilled, pour into an ice cream maker and churn according to the manufacturer's instructions.
6. Freeze for at least 4 hours before serving.

Cucumber and Mint Sorbet

Ingredients:

- 2 cups cucumber juice (blended and strained)
- 1/2 cup sugar
- 1/4 cup fresh mint leaves
- 1 tbsp lemon juice

Instructions:

1. In a saucepan, heat the cucumber juice and sugar over medium heat until the sugar dissolves.
2. Remove from heat and stir in the fresh mint leaves. Let steep for 10 minutes.
3. Strain the mixture to remove the mint leaves, then add the lemon juice.
4. Let the mixture cool to room temperature, then refrigerate for 2-3 hours.
5. Once chilled, pour into an ice cream maker and churn according to the manufacturer's instructions.
6. Freeze for at least 4 hours before serving.

Watermelon and Feta Ice Cream

Ingredients:

- 2 cups fresh watermelon, pureed and strained
- 1 cup heavy cream
- 1/2 cup whole milk
- 1/2 cup sugar
- 1/4 cup crumbled feta cheese
- 1 tsp vanilla extract
- A pinch of salt

Instructions:

1. In a blender, puree the watermelon until smooth. Strain the juice to remove excess pulp.
2. In a saucepan, heat the heavy cream, whole milk, and sugar over medium heat until the sugar dissolves.
3. Remove from heat and let it cool to room temperature, then stir in the watermelon juice and vanilla extract.
4. Chill the mixture in the fridge for 2-3 hours.
5. Pour the chilled mixture into an ice cream maker and churn according to the manufacturer's instructions.
6. Once the ice cream is almost set, gently fold in the crumbled feta cheese.
7. Freeze for at least 4 hours before serving.

Cinnamon and Clove Greek Ice Cream

Ingredients:

- 2 cups heavy cream
- 1 cup whole milk
- 3/4 cup sugar
- 2 cinnamon sticks
- 4 whole cloves
- 1 tsp vanilla extract

Instructions:

1. In a saucepan, heat the milk, heavy cream, sugar, cinnamon sticks, and cloves over medium heat.
2. Stir occasionally and bring the mixture to a simmer. Once the sugar is dissolved, remove from heat.
3. Let the spices steep for 15-20 minutes.
4. Strain out the cinnamon sticks and cloves, then stir in the vanilla extract.
5. Let the mixture cool to room temperature, then refrigerate for 2-3 hours.
6. Once chilled, pour into an ice cream maker and churn according to the manufacturer's instructions.
7. Freeze for at least 4 hours before serving.

Choco-Baklava Swirl Ice Cream

Ingredients:

- 2 cups heavy cream
- 1 cup whole milk
- 3/4 cup sugar
- 1/2 cup chopped walnuts or pistachios
- 1/4 cup honey
- 1/4 cup cocoa powder
- 1 tsp cinnamon
- 1 tsp vanilla extract

Instructions:

1. In a saucepan, heat the heavy cream, whole milk, and sugar over medium heat, stirring occasionally until the sugar dissolves.
2. Stir in the cocoa powder and cinnamon, and cook until well combined.
3. Remove from heat and stir in the vanilla extract.
4. Let the mixture cool to room temperature, then refrigerate for 2-3 hours.
5. In a small pan, toast the walnuts or pistachios with a bit of honey for a few minutes until fragrant.
6. Once the ice cream mixture is chilled, pour it into an ice cream maker and churn according to the manufacturer's instructions.
7. During the last few minutes of churning, swirl in the honey-toasted nuts.

8. Freeze for at least 4 hours before serving.

Apricot and Greek Yogurt Sorbet

Ingredients:

- 3 cups fresh apricots, pitted and chopped
- 1 cup Greek yogurt
- 1/2 cup honey
- 1 tbsp lemon juice
- 1/2 cup water

Instructions:

1. In a blender, puree the apricots, Greek yogurt, honey, lemon juice, and water until smooth.
2. Taste and adjust the sweetness by adding more honey if needed.
3. Refrigerate the mixture for 2-3 hours to chill.
4. Once chilled, pour into an ice cream maker and churn according to the manufacturer's instructions.
5. Freeze for at least 4 hours before serving.

Almond and Honey Ice Cream

Ingredients:

- 2 cups heavy cream
- 1 cup whole milk
- 1/2 cup honey
- 1/2 cup almond meal
- 1 tsp vanilla extract
- A pinch of salt

Instructions:

1. In a saucepan, heat the heavy cream, whole milk, and honey over medium heat until the honey dissolves.
2. Stir in the almond meal and salt, then cook for an additional 5 minutes, stirring constantly.
3. Remove from heat and stir in the vanilla extract.
4. Let the mixture cool to room temperature, then refrigerate for 2-3 hours.
5. Once chilled, pour into an ice cream maker and churn according to the manufacturer's instructions.
6. Freeze for at least 4 hours before serving.

Greek-style Cinnamon and Honey Gelato

Ingredients:

- 2 cups whole milk
- 1 cup heavy cream
- 1/2 cup honey
- 2 tsp ground cinnamon
- 1 tsp vanilla extract

Instructions:

1. In a saucepan, heat the milk, heavy cream, and honey over medium heat until the honey dissolves.
2. Stir in the ground cinnamon and vanilla extract, cooking for an additional 5 minutes.
3. Remove from heat and let the mixture cool to room temperature.
4. Refrigerate for 2-3 hours.
5. Once chilled, pour into an ice cream maker and churn according to the manufacturer's instructions.
6. Freeze for at least 4 hours before serving.

Pistachio and Rosewater Gelato

Ingredients:

- 1 1/2 cups heavy cream
- 1 cup whole milk
- 1/2 cup pistachios, finely ground
- 1/2 cup sugar
- 1/4 tsp rosewater
- 1 tsp vanilla extract

Instructions:

1. In a saucepan, heat the heavy cream, whole milk, and sugar over medium heat.
2. Stir in the finely ground pistachios and cook for an additional 5-10 minutes.
3. Remove from heat and stir in the rosewater and vanilla extract.
4. Let the mixture cool to room temperature, then refrigerate for 2-3 hours.
5. Once chilled, pour into an ice cream maker and churn according to the manufacturer's instructions.
6. Freeze for at least 4 hours before serving.

Mastiha Pine Nut Ice Cream

Ingredients:

- 2 cups heavy cream
- 1 cup whole milk
- 3/4 cup sugar
- 1 tbsp mastiha resin (or mastic extract)
- 1/4 cup pine nuts, toasted
- 1 tsp vanilla extract

Instructions:

1. In a saucepan, heat the milk, heavy cream, sugar, and mastiha resin over medium heat.
2. Stir constantly until the sugar is dissolved and the mastiha is fully dissolved into the mixture.
3. Let the mixture cool to room temperature, then refrigerate for 2-3 hours.
4. Once chilled, pour into an ice cream maker and churn according to the manufacturer's instructions.
5. During the last few minutes of churning, stir in the toasted pine nuts.
6. Freeze for at least 4 hours before serving.

Orange Blossom Ice Cream

Ingredients:

- 2 cups heavy cream
- 1 cup whole milk
- 1/2 cup sugar
- 1 tsp orange blossom water
- Zest of 1 orange
- 1 tsp vanilla extract

Instructions:

1. In a saucepan, heat the milk, heavy cream, and sugar over medium heat until the sugar dissolves.
2. Stir in the orange blossom water and orange zest.
3. Let the mixture cool to room temperature, then refrigerate for 2-3 hours.
4. Once chilled, pour the mixture into an ice cream maker and churn according to the manufacturer's instructions.
5. Once churned, transfer to a container and freeze for at least 4 hours before serving.

Pomegranate and Yogurt Gelato

Ingredients:

- 1 1/2 cups pomegranate juice
- 1 cup Greek yogurt
- 1/2 cup sugar
- 1/2 cup heavy cream
- 1 tsp lemon juice
- 1 tsp vanilla extract

Instructions:

1. In a saucepan, bring the pomegranate juice to a simmer and reduce it by half to create a concentrated syrup.
2. In a bowl, combine the reduced pomegranate syrup with Greek yogurt, sugar, heavy cream, lemon juice, and vanilla extract. Stir well.
3. Refrigerate the mixture for 2-3 hours.
4. Once chilled, pour into an ice cream maker and churn according to the manufacturer's instructions.
5. Freeze for at least 4 hours before serving.

Chocolate and Olive Oil Gelato

Ingredients:

- 2 cups whole milk
- 1 cup heavy cream
- 1/2 cup sugar
- 1/2 cup cocoa powder
- 1/4 cup extra virgin olive oil
- 1 tsp vanilla extract

Instructions:

1. In a saucepan, heat the milk, heavy cream, sugar, and cocoa powder over medium heat until the sugar dissolves and the mixture is smooth.
2. Remove from heat and stir in the olive oil and vanilla extract.
3. Let the mixture cool to room temperature, then refrigerate for 2-3 hours.
4. Once chilled, pour into an ice cream maker and churn according to the manufacturer's instructions.
5. Freeze for at least 4 hours before serving.

Greek Saffron Ice Cream

Ingredients:

- 2 cups heavy cream
- 1 cup whole milk
- 1/2 cup sugar
- 1/4 tsp saffron threads
- 1 tsp vanilla extract

Instructions:

1. In a small bowl, steep the saffron threads in 2 tablespoons of warm milk for about 10 minutes.
2. In a saucepan, heat the remaining milk, heavy cream, and sugar over medium heat until the sugar dissolves.
3. Stir in the saffron-infused milk and vanilla extract.
4. Let the mixture cool to room temperature, then refrigerate for 2-3 hours.
5. Once chilled, pour into an ice cream maker and churn according to the manufacturer's instructions.
6. Freeze for at least 4 hours before serving.

Almond Fig Sorbet

Ingredients:

- 1 1/2 cups fresh figs, chopped
- 1/2 cup sugar
- 1/2 cup water
- 1/4 cup almond extract
- 1 tbsp lemon juice

Instructions:

1. In a saucepan, combine the figs, sugar, and water. Simmer over medium heat for about 10 minutes until the figs are softened.
2. Let the mixture cool, then blend until smooth.
3. Stir in the almond extract and lemon juice.
4. Refrigerate the mixture for 2-3 hours.
5. Once chilled, pour into an ice cream maker and churn according to the manufacturer's instructions.
6. Freeze for at least 4 hours before serving.

Greek Yogurt and Blueberry Gelato

Ingredients:

- 2 cups Greek yogurt
- 1 cup blueberries (fresh or frozen)
- 1/2 cup sugar
- 1/2 cup heavy cream
- 1 tsp vanilla extract

Instructions:

1. In a saucepan, heat the blueberries and sugar over medium heat, stirring until the berries break down into a syrup. Allow to cool.
2. In a bowl, combine the Greek yogurt, heavy cream, vanilla extract, and blueberry syrup.
3. Stir until well mixed, then refrigerate for 2-3 hours.
4. Once chilled, pour into an ice cream maker and churn according to the manufacturer's instructions.
5. Freeze for at least 4 hours before serving.

Karydopita Ice Cream Sandwich

Ingredients:

- 2 cups heavy cream
- 1 cup whole milk
- 1/2 cup sugar
- 1/2 tsp ground cinnamon
- 1/2 cup walnuts, chopped
- 1 tbsp honey
- Karydopita (Greek walnut cake, sliced into squares)

Instructions:

1. In a saucepan, heat the heavy cream, whole milk, sugar, and cinnamon over medium heat until the sugar dissolves.
2. Remove from heat and let cool to room temperature, then refrigerate for 2-3 hours.
3. Once chilled, pour into an ice cream maker and churn according to the manufacturer's instructions.
4. Gently fold in the chopped walnuts and honey.
5. To assemble the ice cream sandwiches, place a scoop of ice cream between two pieces of karydopita and freeze for at least 4 hours before serving.

Cherry and Ricotta Gelato

Ingredients:

- 2 cups fresh cherries, pitted
- 1 cup ricotta cheese
- 1/2 cup sugar
- 1/2 cup whole milk
- 1 tsp vanilla extract

Instructions:

1. In a saucepan, heat the cherries and sugar over medium heat until the cherries soften and release their juice.
2. Let the mixture cool, then blend until smooth.
3. In a bowl, combine the ricotta cheese, milk, vanilla extract, and cherry puree. Stir well.
4. Refrigerate the mixture for 2-3 hours.
5. Once chilled, pour into an ice cream maker and churn according to the manufacturer's instructions.
6. Freeze for at least 4 hours before serving.

Zymar (Greek Apricot and Yogurt) Sorbet

Ingredients:

- 2 cups fresh apricots, pitted and chopped
- 1/2 cup Greek yogurt
- 1/2 cup honey
- 1 tbsp lemon juice

Instructions:

1. In a blender, combine the apricots, Greek yogurt, honey, and lemon juice.
2. Blend until smooth.
3. Refrigerate the mixture for 2-3 hours to chill.
4. Once chilled, pour into an ice cream maker and churn according to the manufacturer's instructions.
5. Freeze for at least 4 hours before serving.

Coconut and Lemon Gelato

Ingredients:

- 2 cups coconut milk
- 1 cup heavy cream
- 1/2 cup sugar
- Zest of 1 lemon
- 1 tbsp lemon juice
- 1/2 tsp vanilla extract

Instructions:

1. In a saucepan, heat the coconut milk, heavy cream, and sugar over medium heat until the sugar dissolves.
2. Stir in the lemon zest, lemon juice, and vanilla extract.
3. Let the mixture cool to room temperature, then refrigerate for 2-3 hours.
4. Once chilled, pour into an ice cream maker and churn according to the manufacturer's instructions.
5. Freeze for at least 4 hours before serving.

Honey and Lavender Ice Cream

Ingredients:

- 2 cups heavy cream
- 1 cup whole milk
- 1/2 cup honey
- 1 tbsp dried lavender buds
- 1 tsp vanilla extract

Instructions:

1. In a saucepan, heat the milk, cream, and honey over medium heat until the honey dissolves.
2. Stir in the lavender buds and simmer for 5 minutes, then remove from heat.
3. Let the mixture cool and steep for about 20 minutes, then strain out the lavender.
4. Stir in the vanilla extract.
5. Refrigerate the mixture for 2-3 hours, then pour into an ice cream maker and churn according to the manufacturer's instructions.
6. Freeze for at least 4 hours before serving.

Grape and Ouzo Sorbet

Ingredients:

- 2 cups fresh grapes, preferably red or purple
- 1/4 cup ouzo
- 1/2 cup sugar
- 1 tbsp lemon juice

Instructions:

1. In a blender, combine the grapes, ouzo, sugar, and lemon juice.
2. Blend until smooth.
3. Strain the mixture through a fine mesh sieve to remove any skins or seeds.
4. Refrigerate the mixture for 2-3 hours to chill.
5. Once chilled, pour into an ice cream maker and churn according to the manufacturer's instructions.
6. Freeze for at least 4 hours before serving.

Cretan Honeycomb Ice Cream

Ingredients:

- 2 cups heavy cream
- 1 cup whole milk
- 1/2 cup sugar
- 1/2 cup honey
- 1/4 cup honeycomb pieces, crushed
- 1 tsp vanilla extract

Instructions:

1. In a saucepan, heat the milk, cream, and sugar over medium heat until the sugar dissolves.
2. Stir in the honey and vanilla extract.
3. Let the mixture cool to room temperature, then refrigerate for 2-3 hours.
4. Once chilled, pour into an ice cream maker and churn according to the manufacturer's instructions.
5. During the last few minutes of churning, add the crushed honeycomb pieces.
6. Freeze for at least 4 hours before serving.

Choco-Hazelnut and Yogurt Gelato

Ingredients:

- 2 cups Greek yogurt
- 1/2 cup heavy cream
- 1/4 cup hazelnut spread (like Nutella)
- 1/4 cup cocoa powder
- 1/4 cup sugar
- 1 tsp vanilla extract

Instructions:

1. In a bowl, whisk together the Greek yogurt, heavy cream, hazelnut spread, cocoa powder, sugar, and vanilla extract.
2. Stir until smooth and well combined.
3. Refrigerate the mixture for 2-3 hours.
4. Once chilled, pour into an ice cream maker and churn according to the manufacturer's instructions.
5. Freeze for at least 4 hours before serving.

Greek Spice Cake Ice Cream

Ingredients:

- 2 cups heavy cream
- 1 cup whole milk
- 1/2 cup sugar
- 1 tsp ground cinnamon
- 1/2 tsp ground cloves
- 1/2 tsp ground ginger
- 1 tsp vanilla extract
- 1/2 cup crushed Greek spice cake (or any spiced cake)

Instructions:

1. In a saucepan, heat the milk, cream, and sugar over medium heat until the sugar dissolves.
2. Stir in the cinnamon, cloves, and ginger, and simmer for 5 minutes.
3. Remove from heat and let the mixture cool to room temperature.
4. Once cooled, stir in the vanilla extract and refrigerate for 2-3 hours.
5. Once chilled, pour into an ice cream maker and churn according to the manufacturer's instructions.
6. During the last few minutes of churning, add the crushed spice cake.
7. Freeze for at least 4 hours before serving.

Greek Yogurt and Peach Sorbet

Ingredients:

- 2 cups Greek yogurt
- 2 cups fresh peaches, peeled and chopped
- 1/2 cup sugar
- 1 tbsp lemon juice

Instructions:

1. In a blender, combine the peaches, Greek yogurt, sugar, and lemon juice.
2. Blend until smooth.
3. Refrigerate the mixture for 2-3 hours to chill.
4. Once chilled, pour into an ice cream maker and churn according to the manufacturer's instructions.
5. Freeze for at least 4 hours before serving.

Strawberry and Feta Ice Cream

Ingredients:

- 2 cups fresh strawberries, hulled
- 1/2 cup feta cheese, crumbled
- 1 cup heavy cream
- 1/2 cup whole milk
- 1/2 cup sugar
- 1 tsp vanilla extract

Instructions:

1. In a blender, combine the strawberries, feta cheese, heavy cream, milk, sugar, and vanilla extract.
2. Blend until smooth.
3. Refrigerate the mixture for 2-3 hours to chill.
4. Once chilled, pour into an ice cream maker and churn according to the manufacturer's instructions.
5. Freeze for at least 4 hours before serving.

Fresh Lime and Olive Oil Sorbet

Ingredients:

- 2 cups fresh lime juice
- 1/2 cup sugar
- 1 cup water
- 2 tbsp extra virgin olive oil
- Zest of 1 lime

Instructions:

1. In a saucepan, combine the water and sugar. Heat over medium until the sugar dissolves completely.
2. Remove from heat and stir in the lime juice, zest, and olive oil.
3. Let the mixture cool to room temperature, then refrigerate for 2-3 hours.
4. Once chilled, pour the mixture into an ice cream maker and churn according to the manufacturer's instructions.
5. Freeze for at least 4 hours before serving.

Hazelnut and Cinnamon Gelato

Ingredients:

- 2 cups whole milk
- 1 cup heavy cream
- 1/2 cup sugar
- 1/2 cup hazelnut spread (such as Nutella)
- 1 tsp ground cinnamon
- 1 tsp vanilla extract

Instructions:

1. In a saucepan, combine the milk, cream, sugar, and cinnamon over medium heat, stirring until the sugar dissolves.
2. Stir in the hazelnut spread and vanilla extract until smooth.
3. Let the mixture cool to room temperature, then refrigerate for 2-3 hours.
4. Once chilled, pour into an ice cream maker and churn according to the manufacturer's instructions.
5. Freeze for at least 4 hours before serving.

Watermelon and Mint Gelato

Ingredients:

- 2 cups fresh watermelon, cubed
- 1/2 cup heavy cream
- 1/4 cup sugar
- 1/4 cup fresh mint leaves
- 1 tbsp lime juice

Instructions:

1. In a blender, combine the watermelon, mint, sugar, and lime juice. Blend until smooth.
2. Strain the mixture through a fine mesh sieve to remove the pulp.
3. Stir in the heavy cream.
4. Refrigerate the mixture for 2-3 hours.
5. Once chilled, pour into an ice cream maker and churn according to the manufacturer's instructions.
6. Freeze for at least 4 hours before serving.

Baklava-Inspired Nut Gelato

Ingredients:

- 1 cup heavy cream
- 1 cup whole milk
- 1/2 cup honey
- 1/4 cup walnuts, chopped
- 1/4 cup pistachios, chopped
- 1/2 tsp ground cinnamon
- 1/2 tsp vanilla extract

Instructions:

1. In a saucepan, heat the milk, cream, and honey over medium heat until the honey dissolves.
2. Stir in the cinnamon and vanilla extract.
3. Let the mixture cool to room temperature, then refrigerate for 2-3 hours.
4. Once chilled, pour into an ice cream maker and churn according to the manufacturer's instructions.
5. In the last few minutes of churning, add the chopped walnuts and pistachios.
6. Freeze for at least 4 hours before serving.

Lemon and Yogurt Cheesecake Ice Cream

Ingredients:

- 2 cups Greek yogurt
- 1 cup cream cheese, softened
- 1/2 cup sugar
- 1/4 cup honey
- 1/2 cup fresh lemon juice
- Zest of 1 lemon

Instructions:

1. In a blender or food processor, combine the yogurt, cream cheese, sugar, honey, lemon juice, and zest. Blend until smooth.
2. Refrigerate the mixture for 2-3 hours.
3. Once chilled, pour into an ice cream maker and churn according to the manufacturer's instructions.
4. Freeze for at least 4 hours before serving.

Raspberry and Pistachio Ice Cream

Ingredients:

- 2 cups fresh raspberries
- 1 cup heavy cream
- 1/2 cup whole milk
- 1/2 cup sugar
- 1/4 cup pistachios, chopped
- 1 tsp vanilla extract

Instructions:

1. In a blender, puree the raspberries with the sugar until smooth.
2. Strain the mixture to remove the seeds.
3. Stir in the milk, heavy cream, and vanilla extract.
4. Refrigerate the mixture for 2-3 hours.
5. Once chilled, pour into an ice cream maker and churn according to the manufacturer's instructions.
6. In the last few minutes of churning, add the chopped pistachios.
7. Freeze for at least 4 hours before serving.

Chocolate-Orange Greek Yogurt Gelato

Ingredients:

- 2 cups Greek yogurt
- 1/2 cup heavy cream
- 1/2 cup sugar
- 1/4 cup cocoa powder
- Zest of 1 orange
- 1 tbsp orange juice

Instructions:

1. In a bowl, whisk together the Greek yogurt, heavy cream, sugar, cocoa powder, orange zest, and orange juice until smooth.
2. Refrigerate the mixture for 2-3 hours.
3. Once chilled, pour into an ice cream maker and churn according to the manufacturer's instructions.
4. Freeze for at least 4 hours before serving.

Mastiha Lemonade Sorbet

Ingredients:

- 2 cups fresh lemon juice
- 1/2 cup sugar
- 1 tbsp mastiha (mastic resin) syrup
- 1 cup water

Instructions:

1. In a saucepan, combine the sugar and water. Heat over medium until the sugar dissolves.
2. Stir in the lemon juice and mastiha syrup.
3. Refrigerate the mixture for 2-3 hours.
4. Once chilled, pour into an ice cream maker and churn according to the manufacturer's instructions.
5. Freeze for at least 4 hours before serving.

Cinnamon-Orange Almond Gelato

Ingredients:

- 2 cups whole milk
- 1 cup heavy cream
- 1/4 cup sugar
- 1/4 cup ground almonds
- 1 tsp ground cinnamon
- Zest of 1 orange

Instructions:

1. In a saucepan, combine the milk, cream, and sugar over medium heat, stirring until the sugar dissolves.
2. Stir in the ground almonds, cinnamon, and orange zest.
3. Let the mixture cool to room temperature, then refrigerate for 2-3 hours.
4. Once chilled, pour into an ice cream maker and churn according to the manufacturer's instructions.
5. Freeze for at least 4 hours before serving.